KV-372-670

The Coach's Guide to Handstands

Index

The Coach's Guide To Handstands
By Will Fraser-Coombe
Artwork By Cole Quigley

Foreword

The purpose of this book is to provide coaches with information on how to teach and correct handstands, and can be utilised by coaches from a variety of disciplines, including crossfit, yoga, callisthenics, dance, and more.

During the technical aspect of the book, it is written as if the reader is performing the handstand. This makes it suitable to be used by individuals who want to learn about doing handstands or coach others how to do them.

This book is a culmination of my own personal experiences and research into the topic.

Without the help of Kieran Wylde of Aspire Parkour and Jason Cheung of Movement Toolbox, this book would not have been possible. They made sure that I could put my ideas onto paper in a coherent way, without over-complicating anything.

Overview

Why Handstand?

There are a variety of benefits to training handstands; from being a great upper body strength exercise to improving blood circulation and lymph flow. They will help improve overall balance, build muscle in the core and upper body, as well as increase mobility in the upper body. Most importantly though handstands are fun and can be done almost anywhere.

Quick Overview

The handstand is one of the most basic and fundamental shapes/skills in gymnastics.
Just because it is basic, does not mean that it's easy; it requires a lot of work to perfect and progress through the different stages of learning the handstand.

The general gymnastics entry to a handstand can be broken down into 5 main sections:

Lunge-   T-balance-   Needle-   Half Handstand- Handstand

Making sure you hit all 5 positions (with this entry) will help ensure you kick up into a good handstand, if body tension and hand placement is used correctly.

Key Points

When in the handstand there are a few key points you need to focus on:
- Keeping 'stacked' with the hands, shoulders, hips and feet
- Spreading the hands to create a wide base of support
- Pushing through your shoulders
- Staying tight in a straight shape (hips tucked, core engaged, eyes fixed)
- Legs squeezed together
- Toes pointed

Prerequisites

To ensure a good handstand and strength for a handstand, I would recommend these prerequisites:
- 30 second dish hold
- 30 second front support hold
- 10 second long front support hold
- 20 second frog balance
- 30 second headstand
- High bunny hop
- 5 correct push ups

Technique

Entry/Exit

There are a few different entries you can use for getting into the handstand such as tuck to handstand, elephant lift, straddle lever and many others. For the purpose of this book we will be focusing on the lunge into the handstand. This will help to further develop skills used in gymnastics and is usually the required entry within grass roots level gymnastics competitions.

As stated in the overview there are the 5 key positions you have to hit in the entry. This is then reversed for the exit, finishing back in the lunge position.

To begin, you want to make sure you start in a solid straight shape (very slightly dished) with arms straight covering the ears. Make sure to keep your head neutral, core engaged pulling the ribs in and hips tucked under. Your legs should be together and squeezed.

From here, lean forward keeping the shape until you feel like you're falling, then take a big step forward into a lunge position. It is important not to lose tension and keep your hips tucked under as this will be difficult to re-correct when you are in the handstand.

Keeping your arms beside your ears and core engaged, you want to reach forward, stretch your fingers away from your toes. As you do this, lift your back leg off the floor so you are in a T-shape. Ensure you maintain a straight back and keep a solid line going from your toes through the body up to your fingers.

Keep this line as you place your hands on the floor into the needle balance. Drive your lifted leg back (still straight) until it reaches vertical. This should (along with pushing with your front leg) lift your other foot off the floor into the L handstand.

From this point you should be finding balance on your hands. Bringing your feet together will be the final step.. When you bring your feet together, make sure you don't lead with the heels as this can result in your feet being driven past the line of the handstand. This will either force you to change the shape or fall out of the handstand.

7

To exit you want to reverse this order (up until the Lunge position).
Throughout the whole process your arms should stay beside your ears and your back straight. Make sure you keep your hips tucked as this is one of the more difficult faults to correct whilst in the handstand. By creating that posterior pelvic tilt* at the hips, it will allow you to maintain a straighter shape in the handstands and build a better connection between upper and lower body.
When coming down, ensure your legs split the same as going up (so if your left leg is the last up it will be the first down).

*This refers to the upward rotation of the hips, which in action is squeezing your glutes to tuck your hips under.

Hand Position

As your hands are the only point in contact with the ground, utilising them in the right way will aid in the ease and efficiency of the handstand.
To do this, make sure your hands are shoulder width apart, with fingers spread to increase the surface area, increasing control. Bend your fingers while trying to keep your palm flat on the floor. This will help you adjust your balance and increase control and stability in your handstand.

To bend your fingers you should focus on pulling your fingertips towards your palm while pressing your palm into the ground.

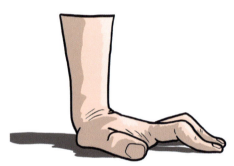

This allows you to exert a lot more force into the ground to help correct shape and maintain balance. A lot of coaches refer to this as 'grabbing the floor', but this terminology encourages athletes to lift on to the tip of the finger and lift the pad of the hand up. This will make it harder to balance using the fingers and can lead to injury.

The final point for hand placement is the angle of the hands in relation to the body. The ideal placement is somewhere between the index finger pointing forward and approximately 30 degrees from the centre line. This will allow for better shoulder flexion and improve body line. This is not a quick fix and emphasis will still need to be placed on pushing tall through the shoulders and externally rotating the arms. By rotating the arms you naturally 'lock' the elbow making it easier to maintain straight arms.

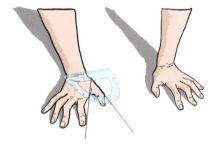

Shaping

Handstand shaping is very important; having the right shape could be the difference between a successful hold and falling. A good shape will also put less strain on your shoulders and lower back which will help reduce injury and make it more efficient.

Whilst in the handstand, you need to follow the key points almost as a mental checklist.

One thing you will hear frequently in gymnastics or any other hand balancing discipline is this idea of being 'stacked'. This refers to the alignment of your joints: wrists, shoulders, hips, knees and ankles, as if you are stacking them on top of each other. There are a few exceptions to this, especially as you progress into shaped handstands but in the straight handstand you want to try and keep to this to make sure your centre of mass is over your base of support in order to maintain balance of the handstand.

Staying tight through the core and keeping your legs straight will help you achieve this. Some cues that help with this is the idea of 'tucking your hips under' which is creating a posterior pelvic tilt. In addition, you want to 'pull your ribs in' to engage the core and avoid arching of the lower back.

To help ensure legs are squeezed tight and straight (and to improve the aesthetics for gymnastics) you should point your toes and squeeze them together. This is a simple cue which will usually help to adjust someone's leg tension but isn't a magic fix. There are a few drills that will help with this that I will come onto later.

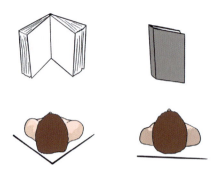

This leads into my next point of body shape in the handstand. Your upper back should be rounded in the handstand rather than perfectly straight, enough to create a concave shape at the shoulders. This will allow a larger base of support creating a stabilising effect, like balancing an open book compared to balancing a closed book. Both can be achieved but one is easier than the other.

When driving the back leg up, the natural tendency is to arch the lower back allowing a greater kick. You should emphasise leading with the hips which will help transfer into finishing in a dish shape. As mentioned earlier this is in part down to the hips being 'tucked' so both cues are helpful for this.

Optimal head positioning is often debated among coaches but generally, there are two broadly accepted positions. Looking at your hands or looking behind you (head neutral vs head out). Both have pros and cons which I will come onto in a later chapter.

The last point with shaping is to push through your shoulders, this will look like a 'shrugging' motion. This will allow you to engage your back muscles and keep your spine straight/slightly rounded.

To cue this to my athletes, I get them to think of pushing the floor away for them and pulling their ribs in. This creates a rounded position of the upper back and keeps their core tight. A lot of the best drills for creating this are done on the floor; not in a handstand.

When most coaches see an arched back in a handstand, they assume that it is a lack of core stability. But, by engaging the core in this position all that happens is the handstand gets moved from a handstand into a planche position (This is due to the closed shoulders so the stacked position can't be achieved).

By shrugging the shoulders instead of engaging the core, you will be able to use the back muscles to pull your body into a straighter position. This will allow the core to engage more efficiently into that stacked position.

Balance Point

Finding the balance point is something that will benefit everyone's handstands. Being unable to find this balance point consistently will result in a very quick plateau in handstand training. As mentioned before, being stacked and having a good shape will make it a lot easier to find this balance point. By having a consistent entry, you will be able to remove the variables when trying to find the balance point. This will be difficult at first as small variations on entry are magnified during the handstand, so it will require a lot of practice.

There are also two types of balancing in a handstand I would like to discuss: Counter-balancing and in-line balancing. Counter-balancing is the use of multiple joints to balance the handstand (which will be discussed in the adjustments section), whereas inline balancing requires balancing through the wrists only.

Both have their uses within gymnastics. For example, counter-balancing will be used more on rings and high bar, where there is a smaller base of support/less stable surfaces. Whereas in-line balancing will be used more on floor, beam, pommel and parallel bars.
In-line is the more desired balance for the purpose of this book as we are focusing on the initial handstand and not yet progressing it.

Even with correct shaping and a consistent entry, there is still one thing missing from the perfect balance point: position of body weight in relation to your hands. Where you place the weight in your hand will make the difference between adjusting your balance and collapsing every time.

13

A lot of gymnasts (especially beginners) have no idea where the weight is in relation to their hands as they don't yet have that intricate proprioception (which I will come to later on). This proprioception is very important in order to have a consistent balanced handstand. When this is being learnt, I have seen many coaches try to correct this by getting the gymnasts to place the weight over the middle of their hands or more towards the knuckles.

This at first seems like a good idea as the hand is compared to a seesaw allowing adjustments both ways. However, in practice, it is very different. This balance point allows for minor corrections, but when falling back down towards where you started, it is a lot harder to correct through the heel of your hand. Successful attempts are usually from counter-balancing rather than in-line balancing as mentioned.

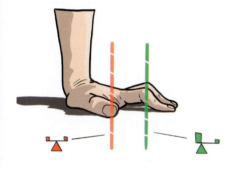

This is due to a greater leverage advantage in your finger as opposed to your heel, so more force can be produced through the fingers adjusting to falling away from the start position and having greater success correcting it. Think of it like standing up, if you lean forwards you can push into your toes to correct the balance. If you lean back onto your heels you have to take a step to stop yourself falling over. The difference is even greater in the hands, as the heel of the foot is behind the ankle joint whereas the wrist is in-line with the heel of the hand.

This means that the weight should be placed more towards the fingers for corrections, almost as if the athlete is always falling forwards and engaging the muscles in the wrists to keep them up, rather than finding a perfect balance and relaxing through the wrists. It's more about control than balance. There should always be a slight element of falling forwards, which you control through your fingers. When you start to feel balanced you relax until you start falling forwards again before repeating. If you put too much pressure into the correction where you 'over-balance', you will end up falling back down which, as mentioned before, is much harder to correct.

Adjustments

There are a few ways to adjust your handstand to stop yourself from falling over. All are acceptable and usually only one is coached at a time. However, I recommend that all 3 main ways are coached concurrently whilst initially learning to handstand. You should base the primary method on severity of adjustment before refining the technique.

You can adjust your positioning through your hands, shoulders and hips.

Adjusting with your hands is best used to make small adjustments, as long as you are in a tight, stacked handstand.

Trying to use your hands for bigger adjustments will overload the wrists in both strength and mobility and either won't work or lead to injury. It also won't work as efficiently if you don't have a rounded upper back as discussed earlier.

For larger adjustments, you want to use your shoulders. This will require less intricate movements than in the hands and provide more strength in the movement reducing the risk of injury. This can be done by shrugging and relaxing the shoulders or by opening and closing the shoulders* for even more control of the adjustments.

*This refers to the extension and flexion at the shoulder joint. Flexion being moving the arm overhead (opening the shoulders) and extension being moving the arm down towards the body (closing the shoulders).

Using your shoulders requires more strength of a naturally weak muscle, so I suggest that a considerable amount of physical prep should be undertaken prior to this. Also, trying to use this for smaller adjustments wouldn't be possible as it is harder to make larger muscles complete more intricate adjustments that you can achieve through your hand and wrists; therefore forcing you to overbalance. It will also affect the shape of the handstand.

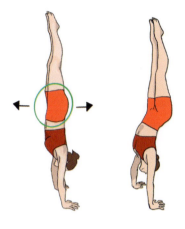

In desperate attempts to balance the handstand it is acceptable to use your hips to adjust the balance. This can be done by piking and arching* slightly. This is good for more extreme adjustments but should be used very carefully and only to regain balance before correcting your shape.
This should not be overused as it can lead to back pain and bad habits which will be harder to correct down the line.

In order to perform a well balanced handstand, it is far more likely and beneficial to do all three adjustments at the same time, allowing for a fluid process engaging the whole body rather than an isolated movement.

*This refers to using the hips for the adjustment. By moving the hips forwards you will create an arch shape, by pushing the hips back you will create a piked shape.

Recovery

When you can't balance the handstand, there are a few ways you can come down safely without hurting yourself.
This is an important skill to learn to help build confidence in the handstand. Without knowing how to recover from a fall, you won't even be able to kick up properly due to a mental block. If you do kick up and fall you are likely to get injured and solidify that mental block.
The 2 main ways to recover a handstand are: forward roll out or twist/pirouette down.

The forward roll out is a skill that comes fairly easy to most gymnasts who can already forward roll. From the handstand position you want to close your shoulders, round your back and tuck your head in. This will lower you towards the floor and keep your head/neck safe. When your upper back makes contact, you want to tuck in the knees to allow the roll out. When used as a recovery, if it helps with confidence, you can bend your arms at the start as long as you have the strength to control the descent onto the upper back. This will assist the roll and take away some momentum. For gymnastics, you will need to keep your arms straight and rely on body control and positioning to build enough momentum to stand up.

The twist/pirouette recovery is more advanced. It involves moving your hands and keeping good core tension to turn around and step down when falling, either stepping out like a cartwheel or doing a full half turn and stepping down like a normal handstand. Most people will step out like a cartwheel as it requires less control and less movement of the hands. I would recommend having good shoulder mobility and stability to do this as it will place a torque-like force to the shoulder capsule*. This won't be a considerable force but something to be aware of. Good technique will mitigate the risk either way.

* This is a twisting force at the shoulder joint.

Delving Deeper

There are a few other points which will come into play in regard to learning how to handstand. I aimed to give each its own title and due attention. These will dive a bit deeper into handstand methodologies, technique and progressing your athletes.

Proprioception

Proprioception is defined as 'your body's ability to sense movement, action, and location' also known as kinesthesia. This is something that is often overlooked when training handstands, something we take for granted, but is crucial to being able to balance and correct shapes. How are you able to correct your handstand if you are unsure of what position your body is in?
There are a variety of ways to improve proprioception, some of which will be discussed in this section.

The first tool I like to use to build proprioception and awareness is to use different situations involving a handstand. This could involve trying handstands on different pieces of equipment such as beam or bars, using different entries into the handstastand; i.e. press, tuck up, lever; or trying different skills that use a handstand such as handstand forward roll, handstand walking or cartwheel.

By using different methods, it allows the athlete to feel a range of positions and motions giving feedback via the central nervous system. By building this awareness it allows the athlete to consciously and subconsciously understand where their body is, and what feels right or wrong.

The next method I use follows a similar concept, it involves changing the shape the gymnast is in during a handstand. I would usually introduce this as soon as they can display a controlled handstand despite how long they hold it. The longer they can balance consistently, the more I will focus on it.

The reason I introduce it early on is to put them in a variety of positions with different balance points, shoulder angles and body shapes. This will give them a better understanding of where their body is and also how to correct balance as well.

You can use as many shapes and positions as you like with some being more challenging than others. To help build up to this point, you can utilise headstands and elbow stands. This will build body awareness without as much focus being placed on holding a handstand, making it more accessible while learning.

This isn't to say that you shouldn't spend time training the shaping aspect of the handstand and neglect fundamental drills. Rather, use these to assist in learning to balance and give your gymnasts more tools in their tool box. Without being able to balance a handstand it will be substantially more difficult to fix the shape, so in the early stages I would focus on training both to get the greatest benefit.

Another useful tool, often used in physiotherapy environments when dealing with ankle stability issues, is training with both eyes closed. Try it yourself, time yourself standing on one leg, either on a solid floor or on a balance cushion. Now try the same exercise again with your eyes closed.
Closing your eyes takes away reliance on vision to assist with balance so you rely on your kinesthetic awareness. It allows you to have better body awareness, and so it is a perfect tool for building proprioception in the wrists, arms and shoulders and will help correct postural sway.
Whilst doing handstand drills get your athletes to do their last set with their eyes closed. To progress them safely, start with supported drills such as the wall handstand, then progress to more dynamic drills.

There are a few technical points which will help your existing proprioception as well.

Firstly, you want to reach your fingers to the floor. This will allow you to both open your shoulders more and place the weight further forwards over the hand as discussed earlier in the chapter.

Next, you want to make sure your hands are down before your second leg lifts off the floor. This lets your body get a sense of feeling through the hands, giving feedback for the kick up into the handstand, allowing adjustments of the entry.

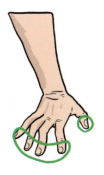 

Finally, you want to push with your fingers as soon as your hands are on the floor. As mentioned earlier, this builds control and keeps tension rather than finding the perfect balance. This requires you to over do the entry to allow for this to happen.

The last point for proprioception I would like you to consider is the training surface. A firmer training surface will allow for easier corrections, while a soft or unstable surface will require more awareness to correct. Both have their uses but be aware of what you chose and why you are using it. Are you trying to get the perfect handstand shape or are you trying to mimic a competition element? These may need different training tools.

What I would recommend is for those in early stages of learning to keep the surface consistent, allowing the body to adapt to the demands you are placing on it, without over-stimulating the Central Nervous System. If an athlete is used to training on a firm floor, when they move to a sprung floor it's unlikely they'll be able to make big enough adjustments through the hands at first. But if you switch from a sprung floor to a firm floor they may then tend to over correct and neither situation is beneficial.

As they then progress and have a better awareness, you can start introducing varied surfaces to further build awareness in different situations.

Proprioception doesn't only affect the balance of the handstand, it also affects the shaping. Holding the legs tight, pointing toes and shrugged shoulders will all need a certain level of proprioception. Time should be spent working on these individual elements outside of the handstand to improve it, working on tension exercises on the floor, and laying handstand shapes using the wall, will have a great transfer into the overall handstand shape.

Having good proprioception doesn't mean they will be able to correct themselves consistently and achieve the perfect handstand. What it will do is allow you to give feedback and them be able to action it. You will probably notice in early stages of learning and development that when you will give a cue such as "straighten your legs", the athlete may struggle making any significant difference. This is partly due to poor proprioception. They may be unaware that their legs aren't straight and it may feel to them like they are. This is where doing specific exercises to build exactly what you want will come into play.

This will affect new athletes and also athletes learning new skills. As soon as you place them into positions or movements that are new, you will have to build and rebuild their proprioception.

Vision

Where an athlete should look in a handstand is a topic a lot of coaches see as preference, either for their athletes or for themselves as a coach. There are 2 main acceptable positions for your head and eyes in regards to handstands which I will cover.

First, the neutral head position, with eyes looking behind you (I often cued the gymnasts to look at where their front foot took off from). This position makes shaping easier especially those with tight shoulders and thoracic spines.

By keeping your head neutral, it avoids a need to arch your spine, which will in turn assist with shoulder positioning and stacking. This may need to be changed later on when learning more advanced handstand techniques. This is a generally accepted method and can help achieve shaping results slightly quicker.

A study by Gautier et al. (2007) stated vision can account for up to 50% of regulation in handstands. This is in part due to the eyes being closer to the visual cue in a handstand when compared to standing. From this research, it was found that the ideal place to look was around 5cm in front of your wrists between your hands. This allows for anchoring, being able to

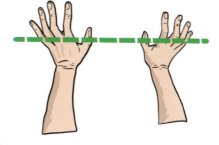

focus on a specific point to regulate balance in relation to body positioning.

Overall, looking at your hands is better and provides more feedback for corrections and balance. However, it can result in gymnasts excessively tilting their head back, which can lead to an excessive arch in the thoracic spine, increasing the difficulty to create an aesthetic shape. So although the 'in line' method is disadvantageous, it has more aesthetic appeal and reduces need for thoracic mobility during earlier stages.

Breathing/Bracing

A lot of gymnasts I have coached have said they can't breathe when upside down. This isn't because they physically can't breathe, but because they are trying to maintain core tension. If they breathe normally, they will lose that tension and their shape will collapse. Additionally, if they haven't learnt to breathe while bracing, it will become more difficult to get that tension in the first place.

This is a skill I have seen most utilised in power lifting to help their body support large loads on their backs. It is often described as 'filling the can'. If you put pressure on an empty can, it will be crushed. But if you try to put pressure on a full can it will stay strong and stable; this is how we should view our bodies.

The first part of this skill is to be able to 'fill the can'. To do this you first have to breathe in fully, not into the chest but into the stomach. As easy as it sounds, it is a skill in itself. It requires taking a deep breath in and filling the stomach before filling the chest.

You can do a self-assessment of this by lying on your back, keeping your back flat and taking five to ten deep breaths, placing one hand on your stomach and the other on your chest. Try to focus on which hand is rising first and making sure you are taking a deep enough breath to move both.

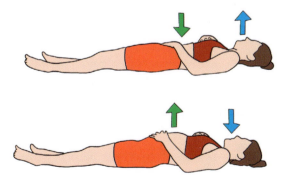

'Filling the can' isn't enough though. Holding this tension throughout the handstand becomes quite strenuous, especially the longer you hold it. So the next part is holding tension while still being able to breath. Taking full breaths will undo the bracing at the beginning and will be almost impossible to regain once it is lost. To maintain the tension, you will have to take short shallow breaths, focusing on only the chest moving. It should be enough that you can say short sentences without losing shape.

This is something you should teach your athletes from early on and use during drills as well as freestanding handstands to help it become second nature to them.

The Handstand Journey
The Handstand Journey

The path to learning a handstand is a journey, there will be many ups and downs and milestones along the way.

The main milestone I focus on with my athletes is reaching a ten second handstand. This is the point at which they are showing a good understanding of balancing and control, you can start to train freestanding handstands consistently, and start influencing shaping mid-handstand. Also, most of the requirements for handstands in gymnastics only need to be held for roughly two to three seconds, so being able to hold a ten second handstand will show that they should be able to hold it for two to three seconds almost every time without issues.

When working towards this goal, I see all drills and methodologies as pieces of a puzzle, rather than progressions and regressions like most skills. This is due to the interconnectedness of the skill as a whole, so with one piece missing, the puzzle is incomplete. Every athlete will have a different combination of pieces missing. Our job as a coach is to

find the holes and fill them with drills that help complete the picture. At times this will involve concurrent focuses.

Along the journey there will be a lot of ups and downs. Like many things in life, progress isn't linear. This is due to all the different systems working together. You may improve in one area and find a weak spot in another, don't be surprised if athletes seem to fix one aspect of their handstands which may seem to become a detriment to another aspect they had no issues with before.

This will cause plateaus in training and will affect the athletes motivation. This is something you will need to be aware of and manage. If it's getting frustrating take a step back and look for other areas to work on rather than get stuck in the loop. It is also important to set small goals for your gymnasts to help keep them motivated, measure progress and praise small wins regularly.

When putting together a plan for your athletes, it is important to think forwards. Why are you trying to get them to learn the handstand? Where do you want it to progress in the future? Is this going to help long term?

This is where you need to choose the methods of training that suit your athletes the most. Exercises that match their needs but also progress to where you want them to go and train in a way that focuses on long term-benefits rather than quick results that require different fixes later down the line. Placing an emphasis on quality and good form from the start will save a headache correcting and fixing other aspects later on down the line.

Too many times have I seen coaches correct something for a quick fix that seems beneficial and may give both them and the athlete false confidence only for it to become a bad habit in the future.

A concept I want to introduce is practice versus play. Practice, in this instance, refers to training close to the top of your ability, in essence, high intensity. Play refers to training in a sub-maximal capacity, an area where you can train for a while with good technique without getting fatigued, so low intensity, high volume training.

The reason I term it practice versus play is because that's how I get my athletes to view it. We do some training that pushes them to their current limit, which will build our strict handstand. Then we lower the level of the drills we do and play around with them. This play becomes less strict and structured to allow the athletes to enjoy the training and will help build exposure to the skill. This usually involves playing games based around handstands, but could be as simple as getting them trying different shapes, entries and exploring what they are interested in.

There are ways to build practice and play together as well. I like to use competitions to enforce this, especially if I am short on time. Handstand holds, max shoulder taps and races are good examples of this. Placing athletes in these competitive environments encourages them to put their maximum effort into each drill and also provides an element of enjoyment from the process.

When starting your athletes on their handstand journey, it's easy to get caught up in pre-requisites. I've even included some in this book, but it's not essential. A lot of strength for handstands comes from doing handstands and appropriate drill selection for whatever level they are at. Conditioning can be built in to fit their specific needs around their handstand sessions. What is important though, is getting them exposed to handstand training as early as possible and not rushing into the harder drills.

So why are handstands hard? What makes them such a seemingly basic skill, so difficult to learn and master? There are a few reasons: First and probably most obvious is the decreased base of support. Your hands are generally smaller than your feet and will be closer together than your feet whilst standing.

This, mixed with the higher centre of gravity, makes it difficult to balance. Balance is the ability to keep the centre of gravity over the base of support. So by having a higher centre of gravity, there is an increase in the lever length, any slight deviance will increase the distance from the base of support.

Another thing that makes it a difficult skill is the unusual muscle use and positioning. In day to day life we are constantly upright on our legs, so to then become upside down and using different muscles makes it difficult to get used to. This is where exposure plays a massive part in learning, the more time you spend upside down using these muscles the better. Be careful though as these muscles aren't used to such intricate movements and aren't designed with weight bearing in mind. They are generally smaller muscles which are easily fatigued, so managing load becomes a very important part of the process.

Lastly, balance is dependent on more joints. There is a much larger system in place to control. When standing, balancing is primarily controlled through your ankles, knees and partially hips. When upside down you introduce wrists and shoulders to the list. Each has a specific part to play in balancing and a lot more focus is needed.

The last point I want to mention with the handstand journey is the importance of using the wall for training. The majority of your training initially should be done against the wall. This isolates what you can focus on and puts less strain on your neuromuscular system, which will help you make more progress in certain areas. This also builds exposure as mentioned earlier. By training against the wall you can increase the muscle's time under tension which is how to build the specific strength needed. If this is neglected and you are only trying freestanding handstands, there is very little time under tension until you can consistently surpass the 10 second mark; before this you are essentially falling, not training.

Programming

Programming is a very important part of learning to handstand. You can do a million drills but without proper programming then progress will be stalled and take longer. There are quite a few points to think of whilst programming, and it will vary from gym to gym and athlete to athlete. Be aware, what works for one person won't necessarily work for another. There are a few principles that will guide you along the right path which you can then deviate.

The first thing to consider is whether you are working volume or intensity. This will depend on the stage of learning and stage of training within the gym as a whole. For performance gymnastics there should be a periodised programme for training. Whether you know it or not your gym probably follows some kind of periodisation. This means that throughout the year there are different focuses of training, and intensity will build up into competitions before decreasing. Below is the basic idea of a periodised plan building up to a competition:

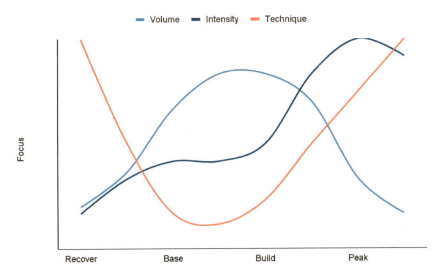

You can see the relationship between volume and intensity in a well structured programme. This can be used in handstand training in build up to a competition, or equally to vary training, increase progress and reduce the risk of injury.

If you are in an early stage of training or learning, the focus should be placed more on volume and as you progress, increase the intensity to achieve the greatest results.

This will then directly influence how many sets and reps (or time) to perform each drill or exercise. In gymnastics, you won't need to go above thirty seconds for any handstand training. This will be more than enough time for a handstand to be held to ensure the athlete has enough specific endurance for the skill in regards to beam and bar routines.

The sets and reps again, are dictated by the stage of training. The higher the intensity of an exercise, the less repetitions you want to complete to avoid fatigue. A general rule to stick by is to base the training off an accumulation of reps. To figure this out multiply the sets by reps to get a number.

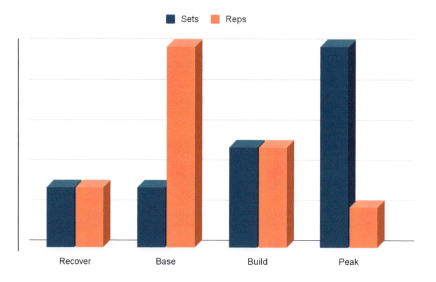

For intense exercises you want to achieve somewhere between 5-10 accumulated repetitions, for moderate exercises around 10-20 repetitions and for low intensity exercises 20+ repetitions. This is a rough guide to help you plan the training but will be a case of trial and error for your specific gymnasts.

The next principle I follow when planning is about how to decide what to focus on. In the early stages of learning, a lot of emphasis should be placed on general strength and spending time upside down. This is where you can build up to the prerequisites listed while still starting to build volume and getting used to being upside down.

Once they get used to being upside down and are successful with the majority of prerequisites, then you can start to focus on proprioception and start utilising the drills and techniques mentioned earlier. Once the proprioception builds alongside volume, you want to start increasing intensity and specific strength for balancing and endurance of specific muscles and positions. Once this has been achieved you can then start to focus on the goal of the plan. This could be the ten second freestanding handstand or introducing dynamic movements or different variations to the skill.

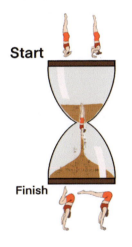

Start

Finish

In essence you should start with a wide focus and the further you progress the more you specify training to meet a goal. Once the goal is achieved you can then widen the focus again, in theory at a higher level than previously started. The more this is followed the more things will open up within training.

The next point to consider is how you will integrate handstand work into your training. There are a few main options which can be mixed together depending on your athletes needs. Handstand work can be included in warm ups and lines, home conditioning, side stations or a dedicated handstand programme. This will all depend on how often they train and time available. Ideally, training should generally be done two to five times a week. This again depends on the stage of training. The more intense the training the less often training needs to be completed.

In a general sense, I would recommend starting with a dedicated in-gym programme to allow you to overview the training and give corrections. As this improves, add in handstand work to home conditioning to allow more frequency and volume of training while still doing some in gym work to check form and give corrections. This can be added into warm ups and lines. As they gain confidence and intensity increases, build it into side stations until specificity is needed. Then dedicate specific time to handstands within the gym programme.

Again, this is a guide and based on my personal recommendations, to find what's best requires trial and error, this should hopefully give you a starting point.

Another important aspect of building a handstand programme is adding in specific tension work. Without tension, handstands become almost impossible, but not all tension work has to be done whilst in a handstand. This can be added in separately in a way that reduces intensity, builds body awareness and will later transfer into being upside down. Tension work can be added in as accessory work around the programme and have more of a focus during the early stages of training.

Another tool that can be used but isn't essential is the use of weight training. This will allow the athletes to build specific strength and load bearing through the arms, back and shoulders. When used properly, it can be a great tool but will need specialist supervision and knowledge for youth strength and conditioning programming.

Rest/Recover

Rest and recovery is important in all types of training, and handstand training is no different. To maximise training, rest should be utilised to get the most out of the training you have done. This is hard to manage when they step out of the gym but there are certain things that can be done in the gym that will help.

First, you should assess your athletes and the areas that need improving. What are their most limiting factors? What is the most important aspect that they need to work on? This could be general strength and technique or a variety of other aspects already mentioned. But more specifically, I would recommend looking at wrist flexion, shoulder strength and mobility and planning accordingly. Finding the weak points will maximise potential and should be a fluid process. No one is perfect and there is always a weak point. As soon as you work on one, another will appear and the cycle will continue. This will help reduce the risk of injury and will be a way to monitor progress and load. There are a variety of tests that can be done, but I recommend some very simple ones that may not be definitive but will give you a rough idea on what to look into next.

The ones I would look at are: Front support lean, prayer stretch, prone lift and wall handstand. This will give a general picture of upper body endurance and mobility specific for handstands.

Something I often see neglected in gymnastics is rest between exercises. Due to time limitations and having such a broad focus, it is easy to try to fit in as much as possible. This can be counterproductive and elicit different traits that you aren't trying to build in your athletes. Rest between exercises allows you to place more focus on specific strength. When the smaller muscles in the shoulder and back become fatigued, larger muscles will take over and compensate. The more you rest the less compensation happens. Between exercises and sets, rest should allow your muscles to recover. For more intense exercises rest should be between 1 and 3 minutes and for less intense exercises, should be between 30 seconds to a minute.

Despite writing the perfect plan, you can't dictate the recovery of an athlete or other stressors they face in day to day life that can impact performance. This is why, where possible, training should be monitored. Any changes to the athletes attitude and performance should be viewed and help dictate their training. Don't be afraid to ask your athletes how they feel and have an open dialogue about their training. This will allow you to regulate their training and change intensity and volume based on the day to day needs of your groups. As soon as you notice form breaking down, don't shy away from taking things back a step and re-evaluating the plan for that day or even that block of training. Knowing when to stop is as important as knowing when to progress.

Coaching

The last piece to getting athletes learning to handstand is down to you as a coach. You can have the best programme in the world but without being able to communicate it and motivate others to follow it then it is useless. Your work as a coach is what will differentiate your gymnasts compared to others.

Giving corrections

Giving corrections is one of the most important aspects of coaching, it is what keeps us in the job. Corrections are vital to coaching but there are ways to approach corrections.

The first point is about focusing on one or two points at a time. Don't overload your athletes with information. It is more productive to give fewer points that they can focus on, than to give many points and hoping they can take some of them on. Once they have listened to the correction and repeated it, showing the correct action that you desire, then you can start introducing more, but do not rush this process. Sometimes it is better to say nothing. Oftentimes coaches tend to fill silence and correct as a way to share knowledge and reinforce their position as a coach. This isn't always needed, some things take time and even if the athletes are looking for corrections, they may already have one to focus on and a simple acknowledgement is more than enough to reinforce a desired outcome.

Teaching your athletes how to self-review is an important skill. Having athletes that can self-regulate and have the awareness to self-correct will save you time in later stages of learning, allowing you to focus attention elsewhere. I fell into a trap before; believing that if athletes self-correct they will have no need for me to coach them; however, it allows me to do my job better as I can spend more time solving problems, formulating plans and monitoring athletes rather than issuing constant feedback. This also builds up a sense of accountability as they are correcting themselves and believe it is their decision on what to focus on. We as coaches are here to guide them onto the correct path.

There are two main methods of self-review I encourage using. The first is feeling;getting the athletes to verbalise the feelings and giving cues to enforce this will help them build an awareness and understanding of their own bodies. Second, I encourage the use of video feedback. The use of video allows them to pick apart what they need to do and help them build an association between what it looks like and how it feels; again bridging the gap of self-awareness. I actively encourage athletes at home to record themselves and review their sets.

There are two types of cues you can give as a coach: internal and external cues. Both have their place and will be used, but I tend to lean more to internal cues. Rather than focusing on the result, I find it more productive to place emphasis on how things feel. An example of this would be: instead of saying "straighten your leg" you can say things like "squeeze your leg", "point your toes" "push tall". By giving them a focus based on feel, you can get them experimenting on how they can achieve this, often finding the desired outcome in the process. This again makes them feel more accountable for the action as they believe it has come from within.

The last point about giving corrections is all about your 'coach's eye'. To build up awareness of what to look for in gymnastics takes a lot of practice, but you have to be very aware of what you are trying to look for. The more you watch the more you will begin to notice and pick up on. Spend time looking at the perfect example, but more importantly, spend time looking at what needs to improve, look at all the little details and know what to look for.

When coaching, especially when starting out, don't be afraid to be wrong. Try and correct, if it doesn't work, learn from it and move on. Try to be confident in yourself, but be aware that you will make mistakes. Don't let it get to you as those you coach will pick up on it and will lose trust in you. Also be aware that no two athletes are the same, what will work for one won't work for another, so work with what you have and keep watching. See how they react to your cues and adjust accordingly.

Progressing

The handstand can lead to a variety of other skills and be progressed in a variety of different ways. This is not going to be an exhaustive list, but will give you some ideas on where you can move on from here. Again I will try to split this into categories so you can clearly identify where you want to progress your athletes and the different avenues you can go.

Different Entries

- Elephant lift
- Pike lift
- Tuck to handstand
- Cartwheel to handstand
- Straddle lever

Floor

- Cartwheel
- Round-off
- Handspring
- Flick
- Handstand forward roll
- Planche
- Shaped handstand
- 1 arm

Beam

- Handstand
- Cartwheel to handstand
- Straddle lever handstand
- Cartwheel

- Walkovers

Vault

- Handspring Flatback
- Handspring
- Half-on

Bars

- Cast to handstand
- Giants
- Toe on to handstand
- Clear hip to handstand
- Handstand pirouette

Conclusion

I hope this book has proved beneficial within your handstand journey, whether as a coach or as an athlete pursuing the skill. With this book comes resources that will help you take this knowledge and implement it into your training. There are a lot of ways to progress the handstand and I will be releasing different content to take you through the next steps, for now take the time to digest the information in this book and start taking action into working to improve your handstands.

"Without knowledge, action is useless and knowledge without action is futile." — Abu Bakr.

Printed in Great Britain
by Amazon

13629060R00025